The Power of Pause

The Power of Pause

Matthew Petchinsky

The Power of Pause: 60-Second Mindfulness Practices
By: Matthew Petchinsky

Introduction

In the hustle and bustle of our modern world, distractions are as constant as the air we breathe. We live in an era where information is abundant, but our ability to focus has never been more challenged. Notifications ping endlessly, to-do lists grow longer, and the pressure to achieve more in less time often feels suffocating. Amid this chaos, mindfulness emerges not as a luxury but as a vital skill—a lifeline to reclaiming our mental and emotional balance.

Mindfulness, at its core, is the practice of being fully present in the moment, free from judgment or distraction. It is not about escaping the demands of daily life but about approaching them with clarity and intention. While the concept may evoke images of serene retreats or hour-long meditation sessions, the reality is far more accessible. Mindfulness is for everyone, regardless of schedule or lifestyle, and it can be practiced in as little as one minute.

The beauty of one-minute mindfulness lies in its simplicity. You don't need to block off significant chunks of time, invest in special equipment, or drastically alter your routine. These practices are designed to seamlessly integrate into your day, whether during your morning coffee, a work break, or the quiet moments before sleep. They serve as tiny anchors, grounding you amidst the swirl of life's demands.

The benefits of these brief mindfulness practices extend far beyond the minute you dedicate to them. By engaging in focused breathing, gentle observation, or a moment of stillness, you can unlock a cascade of positive effects. Mental clarity improves as your mind learns to sift through distractions and concentrate on what truly matters. Emotional regulation becomes more attainable, helping you respond thoughtfully rather than react impulsively to stressors. Over time, these small moments of mindfulness accumulate, fostering a profound sense of well-being.

This guide explores how one-minute mindfulness can transform your life, step by step. It equips you with practical tools to cultivate presence and intentionality, even on the busiest days. Whether you're navigating a demanding career, managing family responsibilities, or simply seeking a reprieve from modern life's relentless pace, these techniques offer a path to greater peace and balance.

In a world that often demands everything at once, mindfulness asks for just a moment. And in that moment, you may discover the clarity, calm, and resilience you need to thrive. Welcome to the journey of reclaiming your focus, enhancing your well-being, and finding serenity—one mindful minute at a time.

Chapter 1: The Science of Mindfulness in Seconds

In a world inundated with constant stimulation, it is easy to overlook the profound effects of a single moment of intentional focus. Yet, neuroscience reveals that even the briefest practices of mindfulness can ignite significant changes in our brains and bodies. Understanding the science behind mindfulness helps demystify why such a seemingly small act—60 seconds of deliberate attention—can have transformative results.

The Neuroscience of Mindfulness: How the Brain Responds

At its core, mindfulness is the practice of focusing attention on the present moment while calmly acknowledging and accepting one's feelings, thoughts, and bodily sensations. This simple act can trigger remarkable changes in the brain.

1. **Activation of the Prefrontal Cortex**: The prefrontal cortex, located at the front of the brain, is responsible for decision-making, emotional regulation, and attention. Mindfulness strengthens this area, enhancing your ability to focus, make thoughtful choices, and manage stress.

2. **Calming the Amygdala**: The amygdala, often referred to as the brain's "fear center," plays a central role in processing stress and emotions. Chronic stress can cause the amygdala to become overactive, leading to heightened anxiety and reactivity. Mindfulness helps reduce amygdala activity, fostering a sense of calm and balance.

3. **Strengthening Neural Pathways**: Mindfulness increases neuroplasticity—the brain's ability to reorganize itself by forming new neural connections. This allows the brain to adapt to positive habits and reduce the influence of negative thought patterns over time.

4. **Boosting the Default Mode Network (DMN):** The DMN is a network of interacting brain regions that becomes active during rest and introspection. Mindfulness helps quiet this network when it becomes overactive, reducing tendencies toward rumination and mind-wandering, which are often linked to stress and unhappiness.

Short Bursts of Mindfulness: The Power of Seconds

Many people assume mindfulness requires lengthy meditation sessions to yield results. However, science suggests that even short bursts of mindfulness—such as a single focused breath or a brief sensory check-in—can create measurable changes in the body's stress response and mental clarity.

1. **Resetting the Stress Response:**
   - The body's stress response, governed by the hypothalamic-pituitary-adrenal (HPA) axis, triggers the release of cortisol, the primary stress hormone. Elevated cortisol levels over time can lead to anxiety, fatigue, and impaired immune function.
   - Practicing mindfulness, even for a minute, activates the parasympathetic nervous system, which counteracts the stress response. This "rest and digest" state lowers cortisol levels, slows the heart rate, and promotes a sense of relaxation.

2. **Improving Focus and Attention:**
   - Mindfulness enhances the brain's capacity to sustain attention and manage distractions by increasing activity in regions associated with executive function. Short, focused mindfulness practices—such as one-minute breathing exercises—help improve concentration and mental clarity, even in demanding environments.

3. **Building Momentum for Positive Change:**
   - When practiced consistently, even 60-second mindfulness exercises contribute to long-term changes in brain function. Each small act reinforces the neural pathways that

support mindfulness, making it easier to access calm and focus during future moments of stress.

The Transformative Potential of 60 Seconds

Why is a minute so powerful? The answer lies in both accessibility and cumulative impact.

1. **Accessibility**:
   - A minute is a manageable, non-intimidating timeframe. Whether you're at your desk, in a crowded space, or navigating a busy day, one minute is all it takes to pause, breathe, and reset. This accessibility makes mindfulness a realistic practice for even the busiest individuals.
2. **Cumulative Impact**:
   - Neuroscientific studies show that small, repeated actions can have a "compounding effect" on the brain and body. A single mindful minute may seem insignificant, but when practiced regularly, it builds resilience, emotional regulation, and focus over time.
3. **Interrupting Negative Patterns**:
   - Mindfulness in seconds works as a circuit breaker for negative patterns of thought or stress. It interrupts the cycle of overthinking, worry, or tension, creating space for new, healthier responses to emerge.

Practical Insights: Starting Small, Dreaming Big

The idea of transformation often feels daunting, but the beauty of mindfulness lies in its simplicity. Sixty seconds of intentional practice can serve as the first step toward a more mindful and centered life. Whether you're taking a single deep breath, observing your surroundings, or engaging in a quick body scan, you're planting the seeds for greater awareness and balance.

In this chapter, we've explored the scientific foundation of mindfulness and the tangible benefits that even the smallest practices can offer. As you move forward, remember that each mindful minute is an investment in your mental and physical well-being. The journey begins not with giant leaps, but with tiny, purposeful steps—one second, one breath, one moment at a time.

Chapter 2: Simple Breathing Techniques to Reset

Breathing is our most natural and automatic function, yet it holds a profound power to calm the mind, reduce anxiety, and restore balance to our lives. In moments of stress, we often breathe shallowly or erratically, which reinforces feelings of tension and unease. By learning intentional breathing techniques, you can tap into your body's innate ability to self-regulate, creating a sense of calm and clarity in as little as one minute.

The Power of Intentional Breathing

Intentional breathing directly influences the autonomic nervous system, which controls our fight-or-flight (sympathetic) and rest-and-digest (parasympathetic) responses. When stressed, the sympathetic nervous system takes over, causing rapid heartbeats, shallow breathing, and heightened anxiety. Controlled breathing activates the parasympathetic nervous system, which slows the heart rate, lowers blood pressure, and induces relaxation.

Studies show that even a single minute of focused breathing can:

- Reduce cortisol (stress hormone) levels.
- Improve heart rate variability, a marker of resilience to stress.
- Enhance oxygen flow to the brain, boosting focus and clarity.

One-Minute Breathing Techniques

Below are three effective and simple breathing exercises to reset your mind and body in a minute or less. These techniques require no special tools or settings, making them accessible anywhere, anytime.

1. The 4-7-8 Breath

This technique, popularized by Dr. Andrew Weil, is a powerful tool for calming the mind and easing anxiety. It leverages specific timing patterns to regulate your breathing and promote relaxation.

How to Practice:

1. Sit comfortably with your back straight and place the tip of your tongue against the ridge of tissue just behind your upper front teeth. Keep it there throughout the exercise.
2. Exhale completely through your mouth, making a whooshing sound.
3. Close your mouth and inhale quietly through your nose for a count of **4**.
4. Hold your breath for a count of **7**.
5. Exhale completely through your mouth, making the whooshing sound again, for a count of **8**.
6. Repeat the cycle for a total of four breaths.

Benefits:

- Slows the heart rate.
- Reduces stress-induced hyperventilation.
- Enhances focus and mindfulness.

Pro Tip: If holding your breath for seven counts feels difficult, start with a shorter duration (e.g., 4-4-4) and gradually increase as your lung capacity improves.

2. Box Breathing (Four-Square Breathing)

Box breathing is widely used by athletes, military personnel, and high-stress professionals to maintain focus and composure under pressure. Its structured rhythm helps to reset the mind and body quickly.

How to Practice:

1. Sit or stand in a relaxed position.
2. Inhale slowly through your nose for a count of 4.
3. Hold your breath for a count of 4.
4. Exhale slowly through your mouth for a count of 4.
5. Hold your breath for another count of 4.
6. Repeat the cycle for one minute (about four rounds).

Benefits:

- Regulates breathing and oxygen intake.
- Improves concentration and emotional control.
- Reduces stress and feelings of overwhelm.

Pro Tip: Visualize a box forming with each phase—inhale as you trace up one side, hold as you move across the top, exhale as you trace down the other side, and hold as you close the box.

3. The Mindful Sigh

The mindful sigh is one of the simplest and most effective ways to release tension quickly. This natural act of exhaling deeply mimics what our body does to reset itself after stress.

How to Practice:

1. Take a deep inhale through your nose, filling your lungs completely.
2. Hold your breath for a moment at the top of the inhale.
3. Exhale forcefully through your mouth, making a sighing sound as you let go of all tension.
4. Repeat for three to five sighs, allowing your body to relax further with each exhale.

Benefits:

- Releases built-up tension in the body.
- Improves oxygen flow to the brain and muscles.
- Instantly resets the nervous system.

Pro Tip: Pair the mindful sigh with a gentle shoulder roll or neck stretch to deepen the sense of relaxation.

The Physiology of Intentional Breathing

Intentional breathing works by engaging the vagus nerve, a key component of the parasympathetic nervous system. The vagus nerve runs from the brainstem to the abdomen and influences critical functions like heart rate, digestion, and mood regulation. Deep, controlled breathing stimulates this nerve, signaling the body to shift from a state of stress to one of calm.

Key physiological effects include:

- **Lowered Heart Rate**: Deep, rhythmic breathing slows the heart rate, reducing feelings of panic or agitation.
- **Improved Oxygen Exchange**: Intentional breathing increases oxygen levels in the blood, enhancing energy and mental clarity.
- **Reduced Muscle Tension**: Deep breaths encourage muscle relaxation, helping to release physical tension associated with stress.
- **Regulation of Cortisol**: Controlled breathing reduces the production of cortisol, mitigating the harmful effects of chronic stress on the body.

Why Breathing Techniques Work in 60 Seconds

A single minute of focused breathing might seem insignificant, but it's incredibly powerful. The key lies in its ability to interrupt the body's stress response. When stress hits, our breathing becomes shallow and rapid, perpetuating a cycle of tension. By consciously taking slow, deep breaths, we break this cycle, creating a moment of calm that resets both mind and body.

Furthermore, these quick techniques are highly adaptable. Whether you're facing a stressful meeting, navigating a difficult conversation, or simply seeking a moment of peace, these exercises fit seamlessly into your day. The accessibility of one-minute breathing practices makes them ideal for building a mindfulness habit that lasts.

By incorporating these simple techniques into your daily routine, you'll discover that one minute is all it takes to transform your state of mind. Breathing is the bridge between your mind and body—a tool you can use anytime, anywhere, to reclaim calm and clarity. Take a deep breath, and let's move forward into the next chapter with a newfound sense of balance.

Chapter 3: Engaging the Senses for Instant Presence

In a world dominated by distractions and perpetual multitasking, reconnecting with the present moment can seem like an impossible task. Yet, the key to grounding yourself lies right within your grasp—your senses. Sensory grounding exercises leverage touch, sight, sound, smell, and taste to anchor the mind and body in the here and now. By engaging the senses, you can redirect your focus from racing thoughts or overwhelming emotions to the richness of the immediate moment.

The Power of Sensory Grounding

The mind has a natural tendency to drift between ruminating on the past and worrying about the future. Sensory grounding interrupts this cycle by pulling your awareness into the present. This practice is especially effective during moments of stress or anxiety, as it shifts attention away from unproductive thought patterns and toward tangible, real-world stimuli.

Scientific studies have shown that engaging the senses:

- Reduces the brain's stress response by activating the parasympathetic nervous system.
- Enhances emotional regulation by fostering mindfulness.
- Promotes a sense of safety and calm, especially during moments of panic or overwhelm.

Sensory mindfulness is accessible to anyone and requires no special tools or environment, making it an ideal practice for cultivating instant presence in daily life.

1. The 5-4-3-2-1 Technique: A Sensory Reset

The 5-4-3-2-1 technique is a popular sensory grounding exercise designed to bring immediate focus to the present moment. It's simple, effective, and can be done anywhere, making it a go-to strategy for managing stress, anxiety, or overthinking.

How to Practice:

1. **Start with Sight (5):** Look around and identify **five things** you can see. This could be anything in your immediate environment, such as a clock, a plant, or a piece of furniture. Try to notice details—shapes, colors, or textures.
2. **Move to Touch (4):** Identify **four things** you can feel. This might include the sensation of your clothing against your skin, the texture of the chair you're sitting on, or the warmth of a mug in your hands.
3. **Listen to Sound (3):** Identify **three things** you can hear. It could be the hum of a refrigerator, the sound of your breathing, or distant chatter.
4. **Engage Smell (2):** Identify **two things** you can smell. If nothing is immediately noticeable, try smelling your clothing, a nearby object, or simply take a deep breath to notice subtle scents in the air.
5. **Taste (1):** Identify **one thing** you can taste. This could be the lingering flavor of a meal, a sip of water, or simply the neutral taste in your mouth.

Why It Works: This technique systematically engages all five senses, helping to ground your awareness in the present moment. It's particularly effective because it shifts focus away from internal worries to external, observable realities.

2. Mindful Observation: Seeing the World Anew

Mindful observation is a practice that involves focusing intently on a single object or scene, allowing yourself to notice its details in a way you might usually overlook. This exercise is not about analyzing or judging but simply observing with curiosity and presence.

How to Practice:

1. Select an object in your environment—a plant, a piece of jewelry, or even a cup of tea.
2. Spend one full minute observing it closely. Notice its color, texture, shape, and any patterns or irregularities.
3. Engage multiple senses if possible. For example, if it's a plant, feel the leaves, observe its scent, or note how the light interacts with it.
4. As your mind wanders, gently bring your attention back to the object without judgment.

Benefits: Mindful observation strengthens your ability to focus, quiets the mind, and cultivates a sense of appreciation for the simple beauty in everyday objects.

3. Integrating Sensory Mindfulness into Daily Routines

The beauty of sensory grounding is that it can seamlessly fit into your existing daily activities. By intentionally engaging your senses during routine moments, you can transform them into opportunities for mindfulness.

Practical Applications:

1. **Morning Rituals:** As you sip your coffee or tea, take a moment to savor the taste and aroma. Notice the warmth of the cup in your hands and the steam rising from the surface.
2. **Commuting:** During your daily commute, tune into the sounds around you—the hum of the engine, the chatter of passengers, or the rustle of leaves. Observe the scenery without judgment.
3. **Eating Mindfully:** Instead of rushing through meals, take a moment to truly taste your food. Notice the textures, flavors, and smells of each bite.
4. **Shower Time:** Pay attention to the sensation of water against your skin, the smell of soap, and the sound of water hitting the tiles.
5. **Outdoor Walks:** Observe the details of your surroundings—leaves swaying in the wind, the crunch of gravel underfoot, or the warmth of sunlight on your face.

4. The Science Behind Sensory Grounding

Sensory grounding exercises leverage the brain's connection to the five senses to anchor attention. When the mind focuses on sensory input, it becomes less preoccupied with internal thoughts or emotions. This redirection has tangible effects on the body:

- **Activation of the Prefrontal Cortex:** Focusing on sensory input engages the brain's executive function, enhancing self-control and emotional regulation.
- **Reduction of Amygdala Activity:** Redirecting attention to the senses dampens the amygdala's stress response, promoting a sense of calm.
- **Improved Neuroplasticity:** Consistent sensory mindfulness strengthens neural pathways associated with attention and presence, making it easier to stay grounded over time.

5. Building a Habit of Sensory Mindfulness

To make sensory grounding a natural part of your life, start small and integrate it into moments where you're already pausing or transitioning between tasks. Over time, these practices will become second nature, helping you cultivate a deeper connection to the present moment.

Tips for Building the Habit:

1. Set reminders on your phone to practice sensory mindfulness at specific times each day.
2. Choose one sensory practice (e.g., mindful observation) and commit to doing it for one minute daily for a week.
3. Reflect on how you feel after each practice. Noticing the benefits reinforces the habit.

Engaging the senses is one of the most accessible and effective ways to cultivate presence. By grounding yourself in the rich tapestry of sensory experiences available at any moment, you can find calm, clarity, and connection, even in the midst of life's chaos. As you move through your day, remember that your senses are always with you—a gateway to the here and now. Take a deep breath, look around, and fully embrace the moment you're in.

Chapter 4: Quick Practices for Emotional Regulation

Emotions are powerful forces that shape how we experience the world and interact with others. While they enrich our lives, they can also become overwhelming, especially when we're caught in frustration, anxiety, or sadness. Emotional regulation—the ability to manage and respond to emotions in healthy ways—is a skill that can transform how we navigate life's challenges. This chapter introduces quick, one-minute practices to help you pause, acknowledge your feelings, and respond with greater clarity and compassion.

The Importance of Emotional Regulation

Emotions, while natural, can sometimes cloud judgment and trigger reactive behaviors. When left unchecked, they can lead to heightened stress, conflict, or regret over impulsive actions. Emotional regulation doesn't mean suppressing or ignoring feelings; rather, it's about understanding and managing them constructively.

The benefits of emotional regulation include:

- Improved decision-making and problem-solving.
- Reduced stress and anxiety levels.
- Stronger relationships and communication.
- Greater resilience and mental well-being.

Quick emotional regulation practices help you pause, check in with yourself, and reset before emotions take control. These exercises are particularly valuable during high-stress moments when time is limited.

Pausing to Check In: Name It to Tame It

The first step in emotional regulation is recognizing and acknowledging your feelings. Neuroscience shows that labeling emotions activates the prefrontal cortex, the brain's rational center, reducing activity in the amygdala, the emotional center. This process, often called "name it to tame it," can help you regain control.

How to Practice:

1. Take a deep breath and pause for a moment.
2. Ask yourself: *What am I feeling right now?* Try to identify the emotion—anger, frustration, sadness, worry, etc.
3. Say the emotion aloud or silently to yourself: "I feel frustrated," or "I feel anxious."
4. Acknowledge the feeling without judgment. Remind yourself that emotions are temporary and natural.

Why It Works: Naming emotions helps to create a sense of distance from them, making them feel less overwhelming. This simple act encourages mindfulness and self-awareness, which are essential for emotional regulation.

One-Minute Gratitude Practices

Gratitude is a powerful tool for shifting your emotional state. When you focus on what you're thankful for, it becomes easier to put challenges into perspective and counteract negative emotions.

How to Practice:

1. Take a deep breath and close your eyes, if possible.
2. Think of one thing you're grateful for in this moment. It could be a person, an opportunity, or even something simple, like the warmth of the sun or a hot cup of tea.
3. Spend the next minute focusing on this feeling of gratitude. Visualize it, savor it, and let it fill your mind.
4. If time permits, write down your gratitude in a journal or on a note in your phone.

Why It Works: Gratitude activates the brain's reward system, releasing feel-good chemicals like dopamine and serotonin. These shifts in brain chemistry promote positive emotions and counteract stress.

Self-Compassion Exercises

Self-compassion involves treating yourself with the same kindness you would offer a close friend. It is especially valuable during moments of self-criticism or doubt. A quick self-compassion exercise can help you shift from frustration or guilt to understanding and self-care.

How to Practice:

1. Pause and take a deep breath.
2. Place a hand over your heart or another soothing gesture that feels natural.
3. Silently say to yourself:
   - "This is a moment of suffering."
   - "Suffering is a part of being human."
   - "May I be kind to myself in this moment."
4. Take another deep breath and acknowledge your feelings with kindness, without pushing them away.

Why It Works: Self-compassion reduces self-criticism and activates the parasympathetic nervous system, which promotes calm and relaxation. This exercise fosters emotional resilience and helps you approach challenges with a balanced mindset.

Transforming Frustration into Calm Clarity

Frustration often arises when things don't go as planned or when external stressors feel insurmountable. In these moments, a brief reframing exercise can help you shift from agitation to clarity.

The "Shift and Reframe" Technique

1. **Pause and Breathe:** Take three slow, deep breaths, focusing on the inhale and exhale.
2. **Identify the Trigger:** Ask yourself, *What exactly is causing my frustration?* Be specific.
3. **Reframe the Situation:** Consider one positive or neutral aspect of the situation. For example:
   - If you're stuck in traffic, think, "This gives me extra time to listen to music or a podcast."
   - If a project is delayed, think, "This might give us more time to refine it."
4. **Focus on Action:** Ask yourself, *What small action can I take right now to improve this situation or my response to it?*

Why It Works: Reframing shifts your perspective from a reactive state to a proactive one. This practice enhances problem-solving and reduces emotional intensity.

Creating a Calm Anchor with Visualization

Visualization is a powerful tool for quickly calming the mind and body. By imagining a peaceful place or scenario, you can interrupt negative emotions and create a sense of inner peace.

How to Practice:

1. Close your eyes and take a deep breath.
2. Imagine a place where you feel safe, calm, and happy. This could be a real location, like a favorite beach or park, or an imagined sanctuary.
3. Focus on the details: the sights, sounds, smells, and sensations of this place. Imagine yourself fully present there.
4. Spend one minute immersing yourself in this visualization. As you return to the present, carry the feeling of calm with you.

Why It Works: Visualization engages the brain's sensory and emotional centers, reducing stress and promoting relaxation. It also provides a mental escape, offering a fresh perspective on challenging situations.

Integrating Emotional Regulation into Daily Life

Emotional regulation becomes easier with practice. By incorporating these quick techniques into your daily routine, you can develop a habit of checking in with your emotions and responding thoughtfully.

Practical Tips for Integration:

- **Morning Check-Ins:** Start your day by pausing for one minute to identify how you're feeling. Use this awareness to set an intention for the day.
- **Midday Resets:** During a lunch break or between tasks, practice a gratitude or self-compassion exercise to recharge emotionally.
- **Evening Reflections:** Before bed, spend a minute reflecting on a moment of gratitude or visualizing a calm and peaceful scenario.

The Transformative Potential of Small Moments

Emotional regulation doesn't require hours of introspection or meditation. In fact, the small moments you take to pause, breathe, and reset can have profound effects on your mental and emotional well-being. By practicing these quick techniques regularly, you'll build a toolkit for navigating life's challenges with grace and resilience.

Remember, emotions are not obstacles to be conquered but signals to be understood. By meeting them with mindfulness and compassion, you can transform frustration into clarity, anxiety into calm, and overwhelm into balance—one minute at a time.

Chapter 5: Building a Habit of Micro-Mindfulness

In our fast-paced world, finding time for mindfulness may feel like a luxury. However, micro-mindfulness—short, intentional practices lasting just 60 seconds—proves that even the busiest schedules can accommodate moments of presence and clarity. By building a habit of micro-mindfulness, you can create a profound and lasting impact on your mental, emotional, and physical well-being. This chapter explores practical strategies for integrating these brief yet powerful practices into your daily life, emphasizing the compounding benefits they bring over time.

1. The Foundation of Habit-Building

Habits form the backbone of our daily routines, shaping how we respond to life's demands. Building a habit of micro-mindfulness involves creating consistent opportunities to pause and reset, embedding mindfulness into the rhythm of your day.

Key Principles of Habit Formation:

1. **Start Small:** Micro-mindfulness practices are inherently small and manageable. By committing to just one minute at a time, you reduce the likelihood of feeling overwhelmed.
2. **Anchor to Existing Routines:** Pair mindfulness with established habits, such as brushing your teeth, waiting for your coffee to brew, or commuting. This "habit stacking" approach helps make mindfulness a natural extension of your day.
3. **Focus on Consistency:** Consistency matters more than intensity. Practicing mindfulness for one minute daily is more impactful than sporadic longer sessions.

2. Tips for Incorporating Micro-Mindfulness into Busy Schedules

Identify "Mindfulness Moments"

Micro-mindfulness works best when integrated into natural pauses or transitions in your day. Look for opportunities where mindfulness can fit seamlessly:

- **Morning:** Begin your day with a 60-second breathing exercise or a moment of gratitude.
- **Commute:** Use travel time for mindful observation or listening to calming sounds.
- **Breaks:** Take a mindfulness break between meetings or tasks to reset your focus.
- **Evening:** End your day with a brief visualization or body scan to unwind.

Set Reminders

In the beginning, reminders can help establish the habit of mindfulness. Use technology, such as phone alarms or mindfulness apps, to prompt you to pause during specific times of the day. Alternatively, sticky notes in visible locations (e.g., your desk or bathroom mirror) can serve as physical cues.

Make Use of Waiting Time

Waiting—whether in line, on hold, or during a lull—provides a perfect opportunity for micro-mindfulness. Instead of reaching for your phone, try a simple grounding exercise, like the 5-4-3-2-1 technique, or focus on your breathing.

Combine with Physical Movement

Incorporate mindfulness into physical activities to make the most of your time:

- Practice mindful walking by focusing on the sensation of your feet touching the ground.

- Pair stretching with intentional breathing to enhance relaxation.
- Engage in a one-minute body scan while seated or standing.

3. The Compounding Benefits of Micro-Mindfulness

While one minute may seem too short to create change, the power of micro-mindfulness lies in its cumulative effect. Each moment of mindfulness builds upon the last, creating a ripple effect that transforms your overall well-being over time.

Mental Benefits

- **Improved Focus:** Regular mindfulness enhances concentration and reduces mind-wandering, helping you stay present and productive.
- **Emotional Resilience:** Consistent practice fosters emotional regulation, making it easier to manage stress and navigate challenges.
- **Reduced Anxiety:** Brief mindfulness exercises calm the nervous system, counteracting the effects of chronic stress.

Physical Benefits

- **Lower Stress Levels:** Mindfulness reduces cortisol production, promoting relaxation and better overall health.
- **Better Sleep:** Ending your day with mindfulness can improve sleep quality by quieting the mind and relaxing the body.
- **Enhanced Energy:** Micro-mindfulness breaks provide a mental reset, preventing fatigue and boosting energy levels throughout the day.

The "Snowball Effect"

Over time, small moments of mindfulness lead to significant changes:

- Neural pathways associated with attention and calmness strengthen, making mindfulness more intuitive.
- Negative thought patterns diminish, replaced by a greater sense of positivity and gratitude.
- Stress responses become less frequent and intense, improving overall resilience.

4. Creating Personalized Routines for Lasting Impact

Micro-mindfulness is not a one-size-fits-all practice. Personalizing your routine ensures it aligns with your lifestyle, preferences, and goals. Here's how to create a routine that works for you:

Step 1: Assess Your Needs

Reflect on areas of your life where mindfulness could make the most impact. Are you looking to reduce stress, improve focus, or enhance emotional regulation? Tailor your practices to address these needs.

Step 2: Experiment with Techniques

Try different micro-mindfulness exercises to discover what resonates with you:

- If you enjoy structure, practices like box breathing or the 5-4-3-2-1 technique may be a good fit.
- If you prefer simplicity, focus on deep breathing or a mindful sigh.
- If you enjoy movement, incorporate mindful walking or stretching.

Step 3: Set Realistic Goals

Start with small, achievable goals to build confidence and consistency. For example:

- Practice one minute of mindfulness three times a day.
- Gradually increase frequency as the habit becomes ingrained.

Step 4: Reflect and Adjust

Periodically evaluate your routine to ensure it continues to serve your needs. If certain techniques feel less effective over time, experiment with new ones. The flexibility of micro-mindfulness allows you to adapt as needed.

5. Overcoming Common Challenges

"I Don't Have Time"

Micro-mindfulness is designed for busy lives. Remember, you only need one minute. Pair mindfulness with existing habits or use waiting times to practice.

"I Keep Forgetting"

Use reminders, cues, or accountability partners to stay consistent. With repetition, mindfulness will become second nature.

"It Doesn't Feel Effective"

The benefits of mindfulness often build gradually. Trust the process and focus on consistency. Even when the effects feel subtle, know that each practice contributes to long-term change.

6. The Long-Term Impact of Micro-Mindfulness

Over weeks and months, micro-mindfulness practices create a foundation for deeper awareness and balance. While the initial goal may be to reduce stress or improve focus, the ripple effects extend into every aspect of life, enhancing relationships, decision-making, and overall happiness.

By committing to these small, intentional moments, you're not just building a habit—you're cultivating a mindset. A mindset of presence, clarity, and resilience that empowers you to navigate life's complexities with grace and confidence.

Remember, every moment counts. The habit of micro-mindfulness begins with a single minute, but its impact can last a lifetime. Let these practices become a cornerstone of your daily routine, guiding you toward a more mindful, connected, and fulfilling life.

Appendix A: 60-Second Mindfulness Practice Library

This library of 20 one-minute mindfulness exercises offers quick, practical solutions for a variety of situations. Each exercise is designed to help you pause, reset, and bring intentionality to your day, no matter how busy your schedule.

Morning Practices

1. Sunrise Breath

Purpose: To start your day with energy and focus.

1. Stand by a window or step outside if possible.
2. Take a deep breath in, imagining yourself drawing energy from the rising sun.
3. Exhale slowly, releasing any tension or grogginess.
4. Repeat for one minute, visualizing your body waking up with each breath.

2. Gratitude Scan

Purpose: To cultivate a positive mindset.

1. Close your eyes and take a deep breath.
2. Think of three things you're grateful for, big or small (e.g., a warm bed, loved ones, or a new opportunity).
3. Reflect on how each one makes you feel, allowing gratitude to fill your heart.

Midday Practices

3. Focus Reset

Purpose: To clear your mind and regain concentration.

1. Sit comfortably and close your eyes.
2. Inhale deeply, counting to four, and exhale slowly to the count of six.
3. As you exhale, silently say, "Let go," releasing distractions.
4. Repeat for one minute to sharpen your focus.

4. Tension Release

Purpose: To relieve physical stress during a busy day.

1. Take a deep breath in and squeeze your shoulders up toward your ears.
2. Hold for a moment, then exhale forcefully while releasing your shoulders.
3. Repeat this action, focusing on the sensation of tension leaving your body.

Before a Meeting or Stressful Event
5. Confidence Boost
Purpose: To calm nerves and cultivate self-assurance.

1. Stand tall with your feet firmly on the ground.
2. Take a deep breath in, imagining yourself drawing in confidence.
3. Exhale slowly, releasing self-doubt.
4. Repeat, silently affirming, "I am capable and prepared."

6. Mindful Check-In
Purpose: To ground yourself and manage pre-meeting anxiety.

1. Close your eyes and identify one thing you're feeling (e.g., nervousness, excitement).
2. Acknowledge the emotion without judgment: "It's okay to feel this way."
3. Take slow, deep breaths, focusing on the rhythm of your breath for one minute.

During Work Breaks

7. Sensory Awareness

Purpose: To reset your mind and connect with the present moment.

1. Look around and name three things you can see, two things you can hear, and one thing you can touch.
2. Focus on these sensations for one minute, letting your mind rest in the present.

8. Hand Stretch

Purpose: To relieve tension from typing or repetitive tasks.

1. Spread your fingers wide and hold for a count of five.
2. Slowly close your hands into fists, squeezing gently, and release.
3. Repeat the stretch, pairing it with slow, deep breaths.

Evening Practices
9. Gratitude Reflection
Purpose: To end the day on a positive note.

1. Sit quietly and think of one positive moment from your day.
2. Reflect on why it was meaningful and how it made you feel.
3. Take deep breaths, letting gratitude fill your heart with each inhale.

10. Body Scan for Relaxation
Purpose: To prepare your body for restful sleep.

1. Lie down or sit comfortably and close your eyes.
2. Starting from your toes, slowly focus on each part of your body, noticing and relaxing any tension.
3. Move upward to your head, taking deep breaths as you release tension in each area.

During Moments of Stress or Overwhelm
11. Grounding Touch
Purpose: To anchor yourself in the present moment.

1. Place your hands on a solid surface (e.g., a table or your lap).
2. Notice the texture, temperature, and firmness beneath your palms.
3. Focus on the sensation for one minute, allowing it to ground you.

12. Counting the Breath
Purpose: To calm racing thoughts.

1. Inhale deeply and silently count "one."
2. Exhale slowly and count "two."
3. Continue counting your breaths up to ten, then start over if needed.

Creative Breaks
13. Mindful Doodling
Purpose: To foster creativity and relaxation.

1. Take a pen and paper and draw simple shapes or patterns.
2. Focus on the motion of your hand and the lines forming on the page.
3. Let go of judgment—this is about the process, not the result.

14. Color Observation
Purpose: To spark inspiration.

1. Choose a single color and look around your environment for objects of that color.
2. Notice the variations in shade, texture, and form.
3. Let your mind rest on this simple exploration for one minute.

For Social Situations
15. Compassion Pause
Purpose: To cultivate empathy during interactions.

1. Take a moment to focus on someone you're with.
2. Silently wish them well: "May they be happy, healthy, and at peace."
3. Let this intention guide your conversation and connection.

16. Active Listening Reset
Purpose: To enhance presence during conversations.

1. While someone speaks, focus entirely on their words and tone.
2. Notice their body language and emotions without interrupting or forming a response.
3. Take a slow, deep breath before replying, ensuring your response is thoughtful.

For Physical Activity
17. Mindful Walking
Purpose: To combine movement and mindfulness.

1. Take slow, deliberate steps, paying attention to how your feet touch the ground.
2. Synchronize your breath with your steps, inhaling for two steps and exhaling for two.
3. Let the rhythm of your movement and breathing calm your mind.

18. Stretch and Breathe
Purpose: To release physical tension.

1. Raise your arms overhead as you inhale deeply.
2. Exhale as you gently bend forward or stretch to the side.
3. Repeat the motion, focusing on how your body feels with each movement.

Miscellaneous Situations
19. Digital Detox
Purpose: To reset after screen time.

1. Put your phone or device aside and close your eyes.
2. Take deep breaths, focusing on the relief of stepping away from digital stimulation.
3. Notice how your mind feels clearer with each breath.

20. Energy Boost
Purpose: To refresh during a midday slump.

1. Stand up and take a deep breath while reaching your arms overhead.
2. Exhale and gently shake out your hands, arms, and legs.
3. Repeat, imagining tension and fatigue leaving your body with each movement.

This library of one-minute mindfulness practices empowers you to bring presence, calm, and intention into every moment of your day. Choose the exercises that resonate with you and adapt them to your needs, creating a toolkit of mindfulness strategies to support you in any situation.

Appendix B: Tools and Resources for Mindfulness on the Go

Building a mindfulness practice becomes more manageable when you have the right tools and resources at your fingertips. This appendix offers recommendations for apps, timers, printable resources, and prompts designed to support your mindfulness journey. These tools are tailored for busy lives, enabling you to integrate mindfulness into your daily routine with ease and consistency.

1. Recommended Apps for Mindfulness Practice

a. Insight Timer

Features:

- Thousands of guided meditations for different lengths and purposes, including one-minute sessions.
- Customizable meditation timer with soothing sounds.
- Community features like groups and live meditation events.
  Why Use It: The app's flexibility and extensive library make it ideal for beginners and experienced practitioners alike.

b. Calm

Features:

- Short mindfulness practices, including breathing exercises and body scans.
- Sleep stories and soundscapes to aid relaxation.
- Daily mindfulness reminders.
  Why Use It: Perfect for those looking to incorporate mindfulness into sleep and stress management.

c. Headspace
Features:

- Bite-sized mindfulness exercises designed for busy schedules.
- Focus-specific sessions, such as calming anxiety or boosting creativity.
- Animated explanations of mindfulness concepts.
  Why Use It: Great for structured mindfulness programs and learning the basics.

d. Breathe+
Features:

- Simple, visually engaging breathing exercises.
- Customizable breath timers for practices like 4-7-8 breathing and box breathing.
  Why Use It: Ideal for those focusing on breathing techniques to manage stress.

e. Reflectly
Features:

- Guided journaling prompts for mindfulness and gratitude.
- Mood tracking to help identify patterns and triggers.
  Why Use It: Combines mindfulness with emotional reflection and personal growth.

2. Timers for Mindfulness

Using a timer can help you stay focused during one-minute practices without worrying about the clock. Here are some timer options:

a. Pomodoro Timers

Pomodoro timers, traditionally used for work intervals, can be repurposed for mindfulness breaks. Many apps like *Focus Booster* or *Tomato Timer* offer flexibility for one-minute mindfulness sessions.

b. Dedicated Mindfulness Timers

- **Zenso Timer:** A minimalist app with customizable intervals and soothing tones to signal the start and end of mindfulness practices.
- **Meditation Timer by Studio 5:** Offers pre-set and custom session lengths with calming sounds.

c. Smart Assistants

Use built-in timers on smart assistants like Siri, Alexa, or Google Assistant. Simply say, "Set a one-minute timer," and focus on your practice without distractions.

3. Prompts for On-the-Go Mindfulness

Mindfulness prompts can be helpful for sparking intention and guiding your practice. Here are some prompts you can use throughout the day:

Morning Prompts

- *What is one thing I'm grateful for as I begin my day?*
- *What intention can I set for today to stay present and focused?*

Midday Prompts

- *What sensations am I noticing in my body right now?*
- *What is one thing I can let go of to feel lighter?*

Evening Prompts

- *What is one positive moment I experienced today?*
- *How does my body feel as I prepare for rest?*

Stressful Moments

- *What emotion am I feeling right now, and where do I feel it in my body?*
- *What is one small action I can take to feel calmer?*

4. Printable Mindfulness Reminder Cards

How to Use:

Print these cards and place them in areas where you'll see them frequently, such as your desk, mirror, car, or refrigerator. Each card includes a simple mindfulness prompt or practice.

Examples of Reminder Cards:

- "Pause. Take one deep breath and feel your feet on the ground."
- "Notice three things you can see, two things you can hear, and one thing you can feel."
- "Inhale calm, exhale tension."
- "This moment is enough. Just breathe."
- "Where is your mind right now? Gently bring it back to the present."

5. Mindfulness Trackers

Consistency is key to building a mindfulness habit. A mindfulness tracker can help you stay accountable and reflect on your progress. Below are printable and app-based options:

Printable Trackers

1. **Daily Mindfulness Tracker**
   - A simple grid with spaces to mark each day you practice mindfulness.
   - Include sections to note which techniques you used and how you felt afterward.
2. **Mood and Mindfulness Tracker**
   - Track your mood before and after each mindfulness session.
   - Identify patterns and which practices are most effective for you.
3. **Weekly Reflection Tracker**
   - Prompts to reflect on your week, such as:
     - *What worked well this week?*
     - *Which mindfulness practice felt the most beneficial?*
     - *What will I focus on next week?*

App-Based Trackers

- **Streaks:** Encourages consistency by tracking daily habits, including mindfulness practices.
- **Habitica:** Gamifies habit tracking, turning your progress into a fun, rewarding experience.
- **Daylio:** Combines mood tracking with habit tracking to identify how mindfulness affects your overall well-being.

6. Additional Resources
Books on Mindfulness

- *"The Miracle of Mindfulness"* by Thich Nhat Hanh
- *"10% Happier"* by Dan Harris
- *"Mindfulness for Beginners"* by Jon Kabat-Zinn

Podcasts

- **"On Being"** with Krista Tippett: Explores mindfulness and meaning in everyday life.
- **"The Daily Meditation Podcast"**: Short, practical mindfulness exercises.
- **"Mindful Living with Athea Davis"**: Focuses on integrating mindfulness into busy lives.

7. Final Tips for Mindfulness on the Go

- **Keep It Simple:** Remember, mindfulness doesn't have to be complicated. A single deep breath can be a powerful reset.
- **Stay Flexible:** If one tool or practice doesn't resonate, experiment with others until you find what works for you.
- **Celebrate Progress:** Acknowledge even the smallest steps toward mindfulness as meaningful achievements.

With these tools and resources, you're equipped to bring mindfulness into your daily life, no matter where you are or what you're doing. Let them serve as gentle reminders that presence, peace, and clarity are always within reach.

<u>Message from the Author:</u>

I hope you enjoyed this book, I love astrology and knew there was not a book such as this out on the shelf. I love metaphysical items as well. Please check out my other books:

-Life of Government Benefits

-My life of Hell

-My life with Hydrocephalus

-Red Sky

-World Domination:Woman's rule

-World Domination:Woman's Rule 2: The War

-Life and Banishment of Apophis: book 1

-The Kidney Friendly Diet

-The Ultimate Hemp Cookbook

-Creating a Dispensary(legally)

-Cleanliness throughout life: the importance of showering from childhood to adulthood.

-Strong Roots: The Risks of Overcoddling children

-Hemp Horoscopes: Cosmic Insights and Earthly Healing

- Celestial Hemp Navigating the Zodiac: Through the Green Cosmos

-Astrological Hemp: Aligning The Stars with Earth's Ancient Herb

-The Astrological Guide to Hemp: Stars, Signs, and Sacred Leaves

-Green Growth: Innovative Marketing Strategies for your Hemp Products and Dispensary

-Cosmic Cannabis

-Astrological Munchies

-Henry The Hemp

-Zodiacal Roots: The Astrological Soul Of Hemp

- **Green Constellations: Intersection of Hemp and Zodiac**

-Hemp in The Houses: An astrological Adventure Through The Cannabis Galaxy

-Galactic Ganja Guide

Heavenly Hemp

Zodiac Leaves

Doctor Who Astrology

Cannastrology

Stellar Satvias and Cosmic Indicas

<u>Celestial Cannabis: A Zodiac Journey</u>

AstroHerbology: The Sky and The Soil: Volume 1

AstroHerbology:Celestial Cannabis:Volume 2

Cosmic Cannabis Cultivation

The Starry Guide to Herbal Harmony: Volume 1

The Starry Guide to Herbal Harmony: Cannabis Universe: Volume 2

Yugioh Astrology: Astrological Guide to Deck, Duels and more

Nightmare Mansion: Echoes of The Abyss

Nightmare Mansion 2: Legacy of Shadows

Nightmare Mansion 3: Shadows of the Forgotten

Nightmare Mansion 4: Echoes of the Damned

The Life and Banishment of Apophis: Book 2

Nightmare Mansion: Halls of Despair

<u>Healing with Herb: Cannabis and Hydrocephalus</u>

<u>Planetary Pot: Aligning with Astrological Herbs: Volume 1</u>

Fast Track to Freedom: 30 Days to Financial Independence Using AI, Assets, and Agile Hustles

<u>Cosmic Hemp Pathways</u>

How to Become Financially Free in 30 Days: 10,000 Paths to Prosperity

Zodiacal Herbage: Astrological Insights: Volume 1

Nightmare Mansion: Whispers in the Walls

The Daleks Invade Atlantis

Henry the hemp and Hydrocephalus

10X The Kidney Friendly Diet

Cannabis Universe: Adult coloring book

Hemp Astrology: The Healing Power of the Stars

Zodiacal Herbage: Astrological Insights: Cannabis Universe: Volume 2

<u>Planetary Pot: Aligning with Astrological Herbs: Cannabis Universes: Volume 2</u>

Doctor Who Meets the Replicators and SG-1: The Ultimate Battle for Survival

Nightmare Mansion: Curse of the Blood Moon

<u>The Celestial Stoner: A Guide to the Zodiac</u>

Cosmic Pleasures: Sex Toy Astrology for Every Sign

Hydrocephalus Astrology: Navigating the Stars and Healing Waters

Lapis and the Mischievous Chocolate Bar

Celestial Positions: Sexual Astrology for Every Sign

Apophis's Shadow Work Journal: : A Journey of Self-Discovery and Healing

Kinky Cosmos: Sexual Kink Astrology for Every Sign

Digital Cosmos: The Astrological Digimon Compendium

Stellar Seeds: The Cosmic Guide to Growing with Astrology

Apophis's Daily Gratitude Journal

Cat Astrology: Feline Mysteries of the Cosmos

The Cosmic Kama Sutra: An Astrological Guide to Sexual Positions

Unleash Your Potential: A Guided Journal Powered by AI Insights

Whispers of the Enchanted Grove

Cosmic Pleasures: An Astrological Guide to Sexual Kinks

369, 12 Manifestation Journal

Whisper of the nocturne journal(blank journal for writing or drawing)

The Boogey Book

Locked In Reflection: A Chastity Journey Through Locktober

Generating Wealth Quickly:

How to Generate $100,000 in 24 Hours

Star Magic: Harness the Power of the Universe

The Flatulence Chronicles: A Fart Journal for Self-Discovery

The Doctor and The Death Moth

Seize the Day: A Personal Seizure Tracking Journal

The Ultimate Boogeyman Safari: A Journey into the Boogie World and Beyond

Whispers of Samhain: 1,000 Spells of Love, Luck, and Lunar Magic: Samhain Spell Book

Apophis's guides:

Witch's Spellbook Crafting Guide for Halloween

<u>Frost & Flame: The Enchanted Yule Grimoire of 1000 Winter Spells</u>

<u>The Ultimate Boogey Goo Guide & Spooky Activities for Halloween Fun</u>

Harmony of the Scales: A Libra's Spellcraft for Balance and Beauty

The Enchanted Advent: 36 Days of Christmas Wonders

Nightmare Mansion: The Labyrinth of Screams

Harvest of Enchantment: 1,000 Spells of Gratitude, Love, and Fortune for Thanksgiving

The Boogey Chronicles: A Journal of Nightly Encounters and Shadowy Secrets

The 12 Days of Financial Freedom: A Step-by-Step Christmas Countdown to Transform Your Finances

Sigil of the Eternal Spiral Blank Journal

A Christmas Feast: Timeless Recipes for Every Meal

The Starlight Sleigh: A Holiday Journey

Elf Secrets: The True Magic of the North Pole

Candy Cane Conjurations

Cooking with Kids: Recipes Under 20 Minutes

Doctor Who: The TARDIS Confiscation

The Anxiety First Aid Kit: Quick Tools to Calm Your Mind

Frosty Whispers: A Winter's Tale

The Infinite Key: Unlocking the Secrets to Prosperity, Resilience, and Purpose

The Grasping Void: Why You'll Regret This Purchase

Astrology for Busy Bees: Star Signs Simplified

The Instant Focus Formula: Cut Through the Noise

The Secret Language of Colors: Unlocking the Emotional Codes

Sacred Fossil Chronicles: Blank Journal

The Christmas Cottage Miracle

Feeding Frenzy: Graboid-Inspired Recipes

Manifest in Minutes: The Quick Law of Attraction Guide

The Symbiote Chronicles: Doctor Who's Venomous Journey

Think Tiny, Grow Big: The Minimalist Mindset

The Energy Key: Unlocking Limitless Motivation

New Year, New Magic: Manifesting Your Best Year Yet

Unstoppable You: Mastering Confidence in Minutes

Infinite Energy: The Secret to Never Feeling Drained

Lightning Focus: Mastering the Art of Productivity in a Distracted World

Saturnalia Manifestation Magick: A Guide to Unlocking Abundance During the Solstice

Graboids and Garland: The Ultimate Tremors-Themed Christmas Guide

12 Nights of Holiday Magic

If you want solar for your home go here: https://www.harborso-lar.live/apophisenterprises/

Get Some Tarot cards: https://www.makeplayingcards.com/sell/
apophis-occult-shop

Get some shirts: https://www.bonfire.com/store/apophis-shirt-emporium/

<u>Instagrams:</u>
@apophis_enterprises,
@apophisbookemporium,
@apophisscardshop
Twitter: @apophisenterpr1
 Tiktok:@apophisenterprise
Youtube: @sg1fan23477, @FiresideRetreatKingdom
Hive: @sg1fan23477
CheeLee: @SG1fan23477

Podcast: Apophis Chat Zone: https://open.spotify.com/show/5zXbrCLEV2xzCp8ybrfHsk?si=fb4d4fdbdce44dec

Newsletter: https://apophiss-newsletter-27c897.beehiiv.com/

If you want to support me or see posts of other projects that I have come over to: **<u>buymeacoffee.com/mpetchinskg</u>**
I post there daily several times a day

Get your Dinowicca or Christmas themed digital products, especially Santa Raptor songs and other musics. Here:
https://sg1fan23477.gumroad.com

Apophis Yuletide Digital has not only digital Christmas items, but it will have all things with Dinowicca as well as other Digital products.